I Know Life's Not Supposed To Be Fair

I Know Life's Not Supposed To Be Fair

But This Is Ridiculous

WHAT DO U THINK??!??

Some real life issues with thought provoking perspectives

Karl V. Farmer Sr.

To order additional copies of this book, contact:
Xlibris Corporation
1-888-795-4274
www.Xlibris.com
Orders@Xlibris.com
89485

Contents

I dedicate this book to my parents Clara and Oscar Farmer. Dad pasted in 1998 mom is still kicking at 88 years old. They were the biggest inspiration of my life. Not perfect people, none of us are, but they believed in and taught us the true meaning of life. We were brought up in the church; honesty, integrity and education were essential. Dad frequently said "it matters not whether you win or lose but how you play the game". Mom's actions showed us that hatred was a waste of time.

A secondary dedication to Dominic, thanks for the push.

I am one of the baby boomers. Born (1947) and raised in the greater Boston area and still residing in the northeast, Hampstead, NH, with my significant other. Graduated from Boston Technical High (1964) and Northeastern University BSEE (1970). I played football in high school and ran track in high school and college. I retired from Polaroid in 2001 after 30 years. The Polaroid experience was a great one. I had the opportunity to work in many different departments and divisions with a host of responsibilities and challenges. Examples: Facilities Engineering, Plant Maintenance, Precision Injection Molding, Robotic Assembly, Product Development and Repair, the Drivers License Team and Camera Manufacturing. I also had the privilege to work on various human resource type projects/committees such as the work redesign team, Affirmative Action Committee and the Computer Integrated Manufacturing Team. When corporate office America decided to start manufacturing off shore Polaroid joined the "party". This eventually led to a reduction in the domestic manufacturing and support effort. In mid 2001 I was told the engineering manager position I was in was going away. I had a choice, a job elsewhere in Polaroid or a severance package that would take me into retirement. I would be a bona fide retiree, I chose the severance. Since then I have worked as a mechanic and gardener at a U.S. Air Force run golf course.

Divorced after 31 years, I have 3 sons and 2 grand daughters. Add in the daughter, 2 grand daughters and 1 great grandson of my significant other and we have quite a crew. This makes family gatherings delightful. The best of it is that they all get along.

I have always been involved in sports. I competed in softball, track and field, bowling, golf, basketball and even played in a father/son game of soccer. During my sons growing years I coached baseball and basketball, participated in PTAs and other school related committees.

As a young child I was very shy but for most of my adult life I have been a participator/leader type. I was the captain of the track team, president of the golf league, a participant on the local community development board and co-chairman of the Hervey Committee (a school organization working with local and state department of education). Chairing and being spokesperson for the affirmative action committee, energy conservation team, and retiree group at Polaroid and being a mentor for the teacher internship program.

My career in the corporate world was a great experience that ended on a real sour note. I started my career as a co-op student at the electric utility company Boston Edison in 1965. I got to work in most of the divisions in the company and upon graduation from NU was offered a job with Edison. They had a professional union, which in itself was interesting to observe, and contract negotiations brought work to a standstill with a strike in 1970. With my first son born and the need for money I took the opportunity to look else ware for employment. Polaroid made me an offer and I took it. As noted above Polaroid was a great experience. Unfortunately the timing of my departure from Polaroid was disastrous. The company was not doing well and a lot of the benefits were eroding. Severance packages were being reduced year by year, the stock was declining and the atmosphere in the company was not maintaining the "family" attitude we knew as Polaroid. I decided to opt out with an early retirement package. The day after I was to receive my first check Polaroid went chapter 11. They cancelled all severance benefits, all retirees benefits and put a hold on most the financial issues of the company. They also had a non-voluntary employee stock ownership plan that put 8% of our pay for 15 years into Polaroid stock. You could not touch that stock until you left the company. We purchased the stock at $32.00 per share; when I left they sold my shares "in my best interest" the said for $00.095 (that's 9 and 1 half cents) per share. Instead of getting $200,000 to 300,000 in my retirement account I got a check for around $300.00. What a great way to enter retirement I thought. Not believing they could get away with this I initiated the process of holding Polaroid accountable. A group of us obtained counsel, got recognized by the bankruptcy court and tested the "highway robbery". To our dismay what Polaroid did may have been unethical and immoral but it was not illegal. The technical term is "we got screwed!!"

The experience was great though, I got to meet some interesting people, got interviewed by TV, Radio, newspaper and congressional celebrities and even went to DC to officially testify at a hearing of the Health, Education, Labor and Pension committee then chaired by Senator Kennedy. It was sad to got to the bankruptcy court in Delaware and have the judge tell us we did a great job, I sympathize with your plight but there's nothing he could do for us.

Strange as it might seem as an engineer my thought preference is logic even though both my parents were as artistic as they could be. Mother was a seamstress, one of the best and fastest at any place she worked. She was also an accomplished musician, playing and teaching the piano and directing the choirs at church. And dad as mentioned was an actor and orator. Both however were athletic, dad played football in high school and mom bowled up to the age of 85. She still plays the piano at her senior citizen day care center.

I guess the artistic side of me comes out in one of my hobbies, photography. I started photography while working at Polaroid, shooting instant pictures of the kids as they grew. I then got into 35mm filming feeling the need to get more creative with my work. When Polaroid got into digital photography I followed suit. I capture, edit and print lots and lots of pictures. My most challenging task and as it turned out my biggest accomplishment was photographing one of my sons' wedding. It was very gratifying when I gave my oldest son the album to give to his brother. He had a puzzled look as he looked through the book. When I asked what was wrong he commented "I paid a lot of money for my wedding album and it didn't come out this good".

Also during this time I had a real passion for golf. As an internally competitive person golf consumed me. I played 2 or 3 times a week, practiced 2 or 3 times a week and subscribed to many golf magazines. I was a student of the game. Goal setting did not have a big influence on me until I got into golf. I wanted to break 100, then 90, etc. then get my handicap to single digits and win a club championship and finally break 70 on my home course. With much diligence and a lot of practice I was fortunate enough to reaching all those goals. I realized shortly after achieving the last goal how important goals are to get to the next level. I scored 69 in a tournament and haven't come close since. I don't play or practice golf like I used to but I greatly enjoy playing golf with my sons, friends and most of all with my grand daughter.

My real passion now though is to travel. Ginny, my significant other, and I take at least 2 major trips each year. We do most of our traveling in the van. This allows so much more flexibility. When we want to stop we stop, when we want to see something off the beaten path we go, if we want to stay long we stay and if we need to alternate drivers we swap. The best part is we travel well together. By car we've been as far north as Canada, as far south as Key West, as far West as Dallas and because we live on the east coast the cape is about as far east as we got. We have also been to California by air and have taken 2 cruises with numerous ports of call. I'm hoping we will be blessed enough to continue this venture for a long time.

Having been "retired" for a while I have taken the stance that it's now someone else's turn to "participate". Unfortunately sometimes I forget and "volunteer" for various projects. Not too many though, I getting to the point where I don't go to meeting or rallies or the like, take no chances.

Writing, actually, finishing and getting this book published is a major accomplishment for the procrastinator that I can be. My next major challenge is to start selling some of my photographs.

Wish me luck. Thank you.

Introduction

I am a Black male who grew up a large urban American area. We lived in various sections of greater Boston, Massachusetts; some poor, some middle-class, some predominantly Black some predominantly White. My primary growing was in the 50's and 60's. Very often adversity would hit, things didn't go my way, or something just didn't feel or sound right. There were times I and others would say; "that's not fair"; "where's the justice?"; "how come he got that and I didn't?" I would be involved in situations or see others get tied up with the injustices associated with the racial and ethnic issues of the times. Most were personal in nature. But there were also many publicized situations that I can recall.

Things like: The teacher always had a "pet". The boss was a mentor to someone else. The evidence points to him, why did I get picked up? Everyone was passing me but I get the ticket. My "baby" sister, the only girl in a family with three older brothers, always got the goodies.

When I ask questions or made observations like; "how come that happened?", "why aren't things happening logically?", "that's not fair!" I often got answers like "That's life", "Life is not supposed to be fair" and most frequently, "Nobody said life was supposed to be fair".

As I grew older and wiser I began to better understand people and some of the things that cause us to behave the way we do. Some of these inequities and inconsistencies took on a new and different feel to me. I began to assess that there were various levels of these illogical happenings. Some I would think were "acceptable"; but some were just plain *ridiculous*. I began to think about writing a book centered around the thought "I know life is not always supposed to be fair, but this is ridiculous". Well this is the book.

This book highlights some personal incidents and issues and happenings I have heard or read about relating to what's fair and what's ridiculous. In writing the issues I also felt the need, or more to the point, the desire to share some of my philosophical views. Thus, there are some "editorial" type excerpts contained in this book.

There's an old adage that says; we spend 95% of our time on 5% of the people. That is to say the silent majorities goes about their lives and businesses without any fan-fair, without, using up "government time" or wasting hidden tax dollars and are willing to accept the "process" and operate within most of the rules. I say most because no matter how "legal" we try to be we all have our little "rule breaking" idiosyncrasies.

But remember, as bazaar as it can get or as "way out" as I can philosophize, there is no question about the following. The majority of the laws, rules and regulations, a high percentage of the judges and lawyers, most of the police, teachers, doctors our mothers and fathers and in general the people in the United States of America are "just" and proper people. And this is by far the best country and system in the world.

Our thoughts have always been a very personal thing. No matter how old or young, educated or not so educated, rich or poor no one can take your thoughts away from you. Thought can be influenced by experience, outside inputs, education and testing. No matter these influences one has the ownership of his or her thoughts.

In between our initial exposure and some time to undertake the experience we are involved in we will go through an analysis of what's happening using past information to form opinions. These opinions can form the way we operate, how we integrate and basically how we live the rest of our lives.

So when someone says to you as they did to me that "life is not supposed to be fair" when you encounter what you think is wrong, you may think to yourself as I always did; I know life's not always fair but this is ridiculous!!!!!

I hope this book provokes thought both now and in the future. Without thought I believe we as people will not survive.

Life

As a young black male growing up in the northeast section of the United States of America I was not confronted with all the "challenges" that were more prevalent in the south. The education system was stronger. Technology was further advanced. There was an arrogance of being "superior" to and more sophisticated than those who lived in the south are. In order to appear more humane and socially superior racial injustices were done in a very subtle manner. The northerners were not necessarily less prejudice than the southerners they were just more "creative". In the younger years there were times when I was naïve to some of the injustices thrown my way. Often, after the fact, things were brought to my attention by others; parents, less ignorant friends, teachers and relatives. Boy was I naïve.

As with most issues, different parents treated the awareness learnings in diverse ways. Some told it all; some hinted at it; some ignored it; others only discussed it when asked. There were also elders who felt the need to let everyone know what was going on; not just their family members but anyone who would listen. And, remember that in those days we were taught "always respect your elders". Virtually everyone had to listen. You did not have to agree but you had to listen. They often would even have their offspring make sure the other children got "the word".

At times our peers took great pride in letting you know how "HIP" they were by preaching the word in the "you mean you didn't know that!" mode. Of course we all knew what was happening. Sometimes they didn't have a clue either.

Then there are the news media favorites. A man shot by a policeman who was chasing him. Seems the policeman was climbing a fence with his gun still in the holster and it ***accidentally*** discharged, injuring the suspect.

In another incident a man received a present from his mother. It was a large picture in a frame. He hung the picture above his bed. Unfortunately during the night it dislodged and fell. Unfortunately it injured his wife. The picture had hit her in the face. She was bleeding. Naturally he grabbed a towel, covered up the wound and took her to the hospital. Before they could finish treating her, the hospital staff had called the police. They handcuffed the man and wanted to charge him with spousal abuse. Even above his wife's' objections. What's he supposed to do?

In still another altercation a man's wife attacked him with a knife. A short scuffle ensued. The neighbors responded to the commotion by calling 911. The man did not want any further escalation so he left the house and went out and sat in his car until the police arrived. They still arrested him. All he did was protect himself and leave the scene to reduce the tension. Is that justice or just plain ridiculous?

Then there are the "experts" who tell you what to do. Starting in the 70's instead of people using their best judgement and making their own decisions, society began to rely on the "experts" to do all their thinking for them. If the lawn needed work, call the landscaper; if the walls needed painting call the painter; let the teachers teach sex education; etc, etc, etc. The infamous Doctor Spock made a lot of money writing a book on "How to be a stepparent". Shortly after the book was out he became a stepparent. As irony would have it, the good doctor could not handle the complexities of stepparent-hood. It is easier to give advice as an expert than to live the experience.

Speaking of experts, have you purchased a lifetime guarantee muffler for your car? No real high initial cost, going to keep the car long enough so it makes economical sense. After a year or so—What's that loud noise? Back to the muffler place with the warrantee. Can you replace my muffler? I have the free warrantee slip. (Reply) "Of course." But we'll have to check out the whole system and make sure everything is OK. We'll give you a call or you can wait for it. Call me please. OK.

The muffler is damaged and it's a free replacement. BUT, the pipes are bad and the clamps need replacing. "What's the cost??" About $150.00 and it can be ready in 2 hours. ***Free replacement??***

Warrantees and guaranties pose their own ironies. If the products are as good as the manufacturers advertise, why then are they so quick to offer you an extended warrantee? They tell you that you won't have to worry. If anything happens you get a no cost replacement. Shouldn't you be entitled to that within the original price of the product? Not forever but certainly for a reasonable period of time.

A most recent story has to do with a wholesale company that issues their own credit card. They send the card applications to you and tell you that you have been pre-approved for credit. You file and receive the card. For the next three or four months you purchase merchandise at the store with their credit card. You receive the bill and in an effort to keep good credit and keep your expenses down, you pay the total balance each time. The wholesaler tells you they are going to charge you a service fee and/or cancel your card because you have paid of the balance. Damned if you do and damned if you don't.

I read a most interesting article in the local newspaper one day. It seems that an elderly couple, both retired, was receiving social security and retirement benefits. The husband received his check one day but the wife did not. They waited a day to see if the mail was just slow. An inquiry to the mailman yielded no explanation or solution. The husband then went down to the social security office to find out why the check had not come. They informed him, after checking the computer, that his wife was DEAD. Flabbergasted the man asks how they got this information so fast, he had just left his wife at the house 15 minutes ago. The clerk informed him that his wife has been dead for over a month. How can this be? The records showed that a hospital, that neither he nor his wife had never been to, CALLED in to tell that she had died. No death certificate needed to be presented. The whole thing eventually got straightened out.

Isn't it amazing how the system allows erroneous information that can stop or prevent your payments to "wander" into their records but it takes a year and a day or an act of congress to get them to input a change that you want entered!!

I got my registration back from the Registry of Motor Vehicles. Because I had been at the same residence for 11 years and had not filled out any change of address forms I assumed the address was correct. My son noticed that the residential address was different than the mailing address. It was **his old** address. After a night to think on it I decided to look at the registration of the other car. This also was incorrect. If you fill out a change of address form, they do not get it right the first time; but if you don't they can change it overnight. I will admit in this case they corrected the error very quickly and without any fuss.

My son was in the procedure of obtaining financing in order to purchase a house. They always do a credit check during this process. Well one of the credit check results was rather ridiculous, even comical when you think about it. It seems one lender had listed him as delinquent by 30 days for payments in January and February of that year. But the report also showed that the January payment was posted on January 27 of that year. And the date of the statement was February 22. How could you be late by 30 days for a payment when the month isn't even over? Don't people pay attention?

When we bought the house we live in now another opportunity for irony arose. The house came with a swimming pool. Not having a pool before I began to investigate what it was going to take to maintain it. Some of my coworkers had pools and provided some good advice. The best information was to read as much as I could about pool care. I did. To give you some background, to keep a pool clean and bacteria free you must add chemicals. Also, there are other chemicals that allow the cleaning chemicals to work their best. It has to do with maintaining the proper pH balance. That's the acid to alkaline ratio. To check these chemical levels you have to take water samples. The owner can do some testing. But there are some more complicated tests that must be done by the experts, the people at the pool store. You know the one that makes its money selling the chemicals. The book said to make sure to do nothing until you got 3 bad readings in a row. A 1-day reading only tells you where the reading is at that time. You don't know if it's low going high; low going low; low staying low; etc.

With this in mind I decide to TEST the pool store. I took a sample for testing. They told me to add some of this today, and then add some of that tomorrow and that should make it good. They wanted to sell me the chemicals. I told them I had some at home.

Well, I did **nothing**, waited 4 days and took another sample to the pool store. They analyzed the water. They told me it was **perfect**. Was I glad I read the books?

We don't even have to give examples of how ridiculous the advertising world is, we have all been duped by them. Just open a package of cookies or potato chips, etc. There is more air than there is product.

In our living, Blacks have another issue that creates a large challenge. The notion of "institutionalized racism". Institutionalized racism causes and brings about inequities and unfairness that usually is very subtle. The main reason is that more often than not, those who are doing it are not even aware that there is a problem. The perpetrators are mostly white males. They are not and have not been intimately familiar with cultures other than their own. They have an awareness of the stereotypes of various ethnic groups. They restrict, select, alter actions, effect pay, impact careers, impose rulings, prevent creativity, disrupt thinking, etc., etc., etc.

In the workplace we have the biggest arena for "institutionalized racism". There are so many opportunities. There are such a variety of subjects, multitudes of ethnic backgrounds and significant organizational variances. This makes it virtually impossible to escape the issue.

I guess the toughest challenge is to assess someone with the stigma of being racist when in fact they can show evidence that they support diversity. They know what the NAACP is or even belong to it. They have hired people of color on their staffs. Often members of their families marry a black or close friends are black. They listen to soul music. Eat soul food. Play sports with the "brothers". They can give you the handshake. Slap you high fives. They're in love with Danzel or Whitney.

All of this, although not intentional, masks the injustices that just seem to happen. When you look deep into the corporate structure you find that Blacks are not promoted at the same rate as whites. Whites hold most if not all the executive positions. There are very few Black CEO's are floating around.

Executive corporate America has its own "institutionalization". This is probably were the notion of institutionalization and the "operating on the inside" philosophy comes from. Remember the golden rule. I bet you remember it as "Do unto others as you would have them do unto you". That's what I was taught. Then someone added " . . . But do it first". But in the real world it's "HE WHO HAS THE GOLD, MAKES THE RULES".

The Board of Directors is a "closed" group. They select and pay the corporate offices, especially the CEO's. Well what do you know!! The BOD is made up of CEO's of other companies. It's the "good old boys" network. You wash my back and I'll wash yours. I'll give you a raise if you get me one. And if we have to fire you, we'll make sure you have enough money to live comfortably for the rest of your life.

If you don't believe this is happening look at the differential in pay between the line worker and the corporate offices. Thirty years ago it was not that great. Then as they "top dogs" got greedy, the efficiency projects became part of the corporate operations. Quality of work life was the thing to do. But as executive pay increased there was not enough money coming in to handle the operation. Companies began to look to do their manufacturing off shore. Labor was cheaper. People would have to be laid-off and or workers would have to take pay cuts. But the "fat cats" still got their share. Now that we've exhausted all the internal efficiencies and work redesigns and downsizing and rightsizing and consolidating the only thing left is to reduce the benefits. The ultimate way to do this is to hire contract, per diem or temporary workers to do the work. Take a good look at the workplace now and you will see evidence of this everywhere. Soon we will have companies with corporate officers and no workers. They will have priced themselves out of the market.

A similar "family" in control of their own destiny is the Senate and Congress. We have to ask, beg, strike, change jobs, change companies, get more education etc to get a raise. These guys vote themselves raises with no opposition.

Speaking of Congress; how about this impeachment issue with President Clinton. One of the golfers at the course I play at commented that he thought this was the *United* States of America. But when you listen to the "debate" you get the impression that it isn't so united. A closer look at the inner workings of the system that controls this country seems to show one of the most segregated entities of all. The gentlemen are on separate sides of the aisle. They do not necessarily vote their conscience but vote the party decision. But it's not called segregation it's "partisanship". Somehow this is supposed to be more palatable. Kind of like the difference between the awful, malicious act of stealing and the "oops" that may be wrong view of embezzlement. The higher you are on the social ladder the less emphasis is put on the crime. I happen to think the opposite; if you are trusted to perform a high level job you should be held more *accountable* and the punishment should be stiffer. But there's the golden rule again.

There is a section in this book that addresses issues of color. But I would like to talk about some of work related issues around Blacks not being in charge. The true issues are sometimes hidden or downplayed. After all many companies have Black VP's and directors. Take a deeper look. Most are in non decision-making, non-production, non-technical, non-financial positions. We are mostly in positions dealing with personnel issues, such as VP or Director of Human Resources. Please do not think that I am demeaning these positions. I am not. These are essential positions and in some companies positions of significant power. The point is that there is a "glass ceiling" effect going on. Again it does not look as though it is being done intentionally, but it is happening.

What also impacts this issue is the "we are more apt to select people that mostly look like me" syndrome. If the people at the top all look alike and there is no variety, how do we expect the top to be as diverse as the workforce? This underlines the need for affirmative action and diversity awareness efforts. But take a look at who's leading the efforts and how they are backed. Or not backed!

How often in your work organization have you seen or heard of a Black person that seems to have been "overlooked" for the next promotion; or has always come out second in the selection process because he or she lacks that one little thing that the white candidate has. Even though the only way to get the experience they required was to have been selected to do a certain project in the past. Who do you think got the project in the past? Of course, he who looks most like the boss. Can you definitely say there was a "wrong" done? No! That's what makes this so difficult do address.

The only way to "prove" or show that this is going on is by examining the numbers. Reality begins to set in. Something is wrong.

You work all your life and never make in a lifetime what athletes or entertainers make in a year. All after you were told "stay in school, with a good education you can do or be anything you want. They offer a young professional athlete a contract for $30,000,000 over 6 or 7 years. The athlete says he feels "insulted" by this ridiculous offer. This is probably enough money to distribute to the poor and put a significant dent in the poverty level. For sure the athlete, his family and the next 2 or 3 generations could not reasonably spend that kind of money in their lifetimes. The fans can hardly afford the really ridiculous ticket prices and the cost of any sports equipment, shoes, balls, sweats, etc. that are endorsed by the athlete. Oh yes, the athlete also gets even more money than the salary for wearing particular sports line of clothing.

One of the most important issues in society today is that of abuse. There are and have been so many negative and harrowing experiences. There are also many different philosophies and feelings about what constitute "abuse". This has created not just inequities and biases but downright hatred. Between families, the sexes, religions, etc. Clearly, the most significant problem has been the loss of lives.

It's hard for me to believe people want to intentionally do bodily harm to one another. But, I know there are situations where this is in fact the case. Thankfully this is the exception rather than the rule.

The notion that people do not INTEND to do each other harm but in fact DO harm others is of the utmost concern. The learnings of our younger years, the impact of our experiences in society, our family upbringing and in general the subconscious effect(s) this has on us all plays some role in our actions. Very often we *excuse* unwanted actions because we are aware of past influences. This can prove harmful in the long run. If we do not hold people accountable for their actions, the tendency may be to continue the "wrong doing" until it reaches a troublesome point.

Holding accountable is not about immediate punishment as much as it is making a person aware that their actions are unwanted. If this is done early enough and tactfully there may not be any further escalation of the problem. If we trivialize the unwanted actions and just let "boys be boys", the problem can escalate to a point of no return.

So far the incidents I've mentioned do not require much interpretation. When the actions are cut and dry and everyone knows what the issue is, you can usually get to a resolution, sometimes fairly quickly.

When the interpretation of actions and/or words is not very clear, the resolution requires much more discussion and explanation. What means one thing to me means something different to others. And not just one difference, it can mean various things to many different people.

This dictates more listening and understanding than both parties may desire to get into. Third party, unbiased and/or professional assistance is often needed. This presents its own set of problems. Who to go to? Who picks the person? Should it be a male or female? Should it be young or old? Can a person not of my race, religion, generation or sex understand my issues? The constraints for an unbiased arbitrator are endless. The need for the arbitrator in order to keep a sound relationship is often the only way.

Actions are even more complicated. They are tougher to "read" and more often than not even we are unaware of how we look or exactly how we sound when we do something. This leaves lots of room for interpretation. The state of mind that the listener/observer is in also plays a big part in the interpretation. If you are in an agitated state to begin with, your response may not be as rational or excepting as if you were in a happy mood.

The tendency we all have is to interpret the actions or words of someone else in a manner that is consistent with what we would have meant by what was done or said. Too often this is the crux of relationships going sour. Especially if a third party gives their opinion of what THEY meant by that without consulting the person face to face.

These are the types of confrontations that can escalate to the "abuse" level. There are various types of abuse. Physical abuse, verbal abuse, sexual abuse, racial abuse, etc. The most difficulty with abuse is determining exactly what abuse is and means. Again as already stated, different things mean something different to others. What's a joke to me is objectionable to you. What is normal language to you is vulgar to me. The variations are endless. The more people involved the more complicated this gets.

Physical abuse would seem to be a straightforward issue. This is so far from the truth. There are definite physical abuse issues. Spousal abuse and child abuse when bodily injury is very evident. However, sound discipline is often mistaken for child abuse. Having raised three sons I found it extremely difficult to determine that fine line between the times they needed "hard" discipline and carrying the discipline too far to the point of being abuse. The fear is that if you "spare the rod you spoil the child". This gets back to accountability. If a youngster or anyone for that matter is allowed to do as they please with only verbal punishment, will they obey the laws when they grow up. I believe this is the main reason that the penal system is overburdened today. Not enough children were properly disciplined in the formative years. I remember Judge Whopner on "People's Court" telling a young mother that "it's barbaric to spank a child in this day and age". He was talking about a 4-year-old. If you can't SPANK a 4-year-old then how do you get him or her to behave? Watch the frustration as mothers and fathers cope with their kids in the malls, grocery stores, etc. Though I agree that abuse is going to far often times talking is not always enough.

A parent disciplines a child with a spanking—no eye eyewitnesses of the issues leading up to the "discipline—CHILD ABUSE an "innocent" bystander cries—DSS takes the kid(s). SHAME ON THE PARENTS. In Springfield Massachusetts a police officer kicks a suspect in handcuffs, lying on the ground being held by other officers. The incident is recorded on a video camera. An investigation is held. What was the result of the *authority's* probe? THERE WAS NO CRIMINAL WRONG DOING!! I guess the rules are different depending on the uniform you wear.

As in the Rodney King case and probably thousands of other cases of questionable police actions against Blacks, the findings are no criminal wrong. In the end, after public outcries, the system usually makes some sort of financial concession. The problem is the public has to foot the monetary burden.

This is also the type of occurrence that gives the youngsters the wrong message. How do I respect authority when I see this happening? And it happens over and over again.

The courts, correctional facilities and jails are full of youngsters. Many of these youngsters have no respect for authority and certainly will not do what they are told or asked to do. If they were not disciplined as children the tendency is to continue on, as they grow up, to do what ever they want. The longer this lack of discipline continues, the more difficult it is to correct it. I am not advocating beating a child half to death nor am I saying you should punish every child the same. Some children respond to talk, some respond to restrictive punishment (i.e. no playtime or TV) and some only respond to physical discipline. This is one of if not the most difficult area to deal with. But again, if children aren't held accountable, the results can be catastrophic in the future.

Wouldn't you love a job like the weather people have. Today is going to be a beautiful day, tomorrow will be a repeat of today and the next day will bring a cold front with some fog and drizzle. The reality—It rains for three straight days and the sun comes out and the last day is beautiful. It's just the opposite of the forecast. Then the weatherman comes in to tell us what went wrong with the weather. If we did that in our jobs, how long would we keep our jobs?

Ever get an appointment for the doctor, dentist or court. What time does your 8:00 appointment start? Maybe they call you at 8:15 to tell you it will be a few minutes before it's your turn. Half hour, 1 hour later you get called again. Is it your turn? No! It's another waiting room. You finally get there and it's lunchtime. How long do you think you can make them wait for you. Try paying the bill late or telling the judge in court to wait while you get something to eat. I'll bet they won't take too kindly to this.

The news media is extremely guilty of adding to the ridiculous rather than fair issue. Just listen and watch a news show. It doesn't even have to be one of the tabloid segments. The "need" to sensationalize has driven them to more than dramatize at least the headlines and lead-ins to the true stories.

They like to leave you in suspense and keep you from changing the channel as they go to a commercial. When the story is finally conveyed you wonder what the lead-in was all about.

Headline in the sports page after a skating competition.

"American beats Kwan"

Well guess what? The skater Miss Kwan just happens to be an American citizen.

And we all know how misleading and ridiculous the advertising world is. The advertisement says "Just 99 cents up to 20 minutes and 10 cents a minute there-after". Well if you make 10 calls that take 2 minutes each; that's a total of 20 minutes. You would expect to be charged 99 cents, but it will cost you $9.99. It's 99 cents per call up to 20 minutes per call. Lots of people have paid the price for this misleading ad.

In large part these issues are driven by the increased competitive nature of the world economy. There are various levels of competition. Friendly competition can bring out the best in us, it can be fun and it can be an effective means to achieving success. But "cut throat, vicious, "win at all cost" competition can be very detrimental and even destructive. I believe we have to be able to communicate the difference, especially to young people, in order to move to a more stable, less stressful and more fruitful society.

Unfortunately the world of computers, voice mail, E-mail, etc. has taken much of the personal, eye to eye, person to person contact out of our day to day communications. Yes it's quicker, more efficient, more precise but is it better? Time will tell; or will we write a program to analyze the problem and generate the solution?!?

Another aspect of "competitiveness" that often brings about the ridiculous is advice or procedures followed in high profile or political situations. Too frequently people get emotionally overwhelmed or overconfident in their position to use common sense. Three come to mind:

The Rodney King case, the Mark Furman testimony in the O. J. Simpson case and President Clinton's handling of the Monica Lewinsky "fiasco".

In the King case the defense implied that the suspect had made menacing and non-compliant movements. This they said justified the police to be able "protect" himself against the suspect. In pleading the case they showed the video of the incident not just in slow motion but also a frame at a time. Even though there is no way that the police could have detected these movements in real time the prosecution allowed the defense proceed without challenging the process. They also did not challenge the officer when he said he was in fear of his life. THERE WERE MORE THAN 5 FELLOW OFFICERS, ALL WITH GUNS AND NIGHT STICKS AND AT LEAST 1 TAISER GUN. He was in FEAR OF HIS LIFE? I don't think I want that person "PROTECTING?" me. The statement went unchallenged in that aspect.

In the O. J. Simpson case I don't know what the prosecutors were thinking when they did not "coach" Mark Furman properly on handling the "N" word questioning. If he had just said something in the manner of "yes I had used the word in the past, I'm sorry I used it but it has no bearing on this case" the defense would have been hard pressed to make the issue out of it that it eventually did.

As far as President Clinton is concerned his advisors should have told him to tell the people that the issue, whether it happened or not, has no effect on the case at hand. The President's private relationships are just that, private. Any question of any sexual relationship on the President's part is a private matter. This should hold true any President and his or her relationship with his or her spouse. There will be no more discussions or press conferences on the matter. I will only answer to the judicial system regarding the White Water case.

There could not have been any chance of calling that statement a lie or for people to have thoughts of perjury.

In these situations I think the people "in charge" get to an emotional state that makes them think or hope the public will believe the **ridiculous**; I guess sometimes we do.

One pet peeve I have is the issue of repaying student loans. The way the government handles these cases shows how ridiculously different the treatment is for the rich and the poor. Let's say a person on Welfare happens to go out and get a menial job making minimum wage or less. With the benefits and the job money they make less than the poverty level. However, if they are caught they are labeled criminals and are often prosecuted for fraud. They are also asked, no, demanded to pay back the money.

A student gets a government student loan to complete his or her education. They graduate as a doctor or lawyer and begin their practice. Remember that in both these fields of work you need to pass a test of some sort or register in some legal fashion. So it should not be difficult to track down and restrict the future practice of these professionals if you wanted to. Well one of the biggest "frauds" of the system now is that too many of these people are not repaying their student loans. They are making certainly well above the poverty level of the welfare recipients but are far less apt to be sought after or prosecuted for their "theft" of the system.

Yes I truly believe there is a double standard. I don't suggest it has to be fair all the time but fairness sometimes seams to be the exception rather than the rule. That is ridiculous.

"Halls Of Justice?"

Probably the most ironic and contradictory entity in question is our *"JUSTICE"* system. We are all told at a young age that if we "keep or nose clean and obey the law" justice will prevail. I don't know about you but I have seen, heard and read too many crazy stories to believe that it's justice that's going on. An excerpt from an article I read years ago states it best. I'm sorry I don't know the exact origination, but I believe a noted criminal attorney wrote it.

THE RULES of the JUSTICE GAME

"These rules seem—in practice-to govern the justice game in America. Most of the participants in the criminal justice system understand them. Although these rules never appear in print, they seem to control the realities of the process. Like all rules, they are necessarily stated in oversimplified terms. But they tell an important part of how the system operates in practice. Here are some of the key rules of the justice game:

Rule 1: Almost all criminal defendants are, in fact guilty.

Rule 2: All criminal defense lawyers, prosecutors and judges understand and believe Rule 1.

Rule 3: It is easier to convict guilty defendants by violating the Constitution than by complying with it, and in some cases it is impossible to convict guilty defendants without violating the Constitution.

Rule 4: Almost all police lie about whether they violated the Constitution in order to convict guilty defendants.

Rule 5: All prosecutors, judges and defense attorneys are aware of Rule 4.

Rule 6: Many prosecutors implicitly encourage police to lie about whether they violated the Constitution in order to convict guilty defendants.

Rule 7: All judges are aware of Rule 6.

Rule 8: Most trial judges pretend to believe police officers who they know are lying.

Rule 9: All appellate judges are aware of Rule 8, yet many pretend to believe the trial judges who pretend to believe the lying police officers.

Rule 10: Most judges disbelieve defendants about whether their Constitutional rights have been violated, even if they are telling the truth.

Rule 11: Most judges and prosecutors would not knowingly convict a defendant who they believe to be innocent of the crime charged (or a closely related crime).

Rule 12: Rule 11 does not apply to members of organized crime, drug dealers, career criminals or potential informers. *(**Might I add BLACKS** and other minorities)*

Rule 13: Nobody really wants justice.

That's quite an array of observations by someone who makes a living in this system. Certainly it's more ridiculous than fair.

A friend of mine's quote from his attorney friend is along the same train of thought. When discussing some legal stories the lawyer noted that "It is not about justice, it's about conflict resolution". Again relating to the "justice" system; we typically expect to be treated in a just manner when dealing within the "Halls of Justice".

How many family members, friends or co-workers have you heard tell of their harrowing and or unjust experiences with the law? When in court before a judge, out in the street stopped by the police, or just doing what we do every day.

Two close friends of our family were out one night attending a movie. They were both males. As they were walking to the car to go home they somehow got separated by 20 feet or so. Some non-uniformed policemen thought the first male looked like a criminal suspect they had been looking for. They approached him for questioning. Thinking someone was bothering his partner the second friend ran up to ask what was going on. Without an explanation one of the policemen hit him in the head with a flashlight. The blow caused a cut to his head. In order to cover up their mistake the police arrested him and charged him with interference and resisting arrest. This was a person with no criminal record and no previous incidents with the law. The case went to court. The law said they would drop the charges if he promised not to sue the police department. The policemen get off with no punishment or reprimand.

The speed or lack thereof with which the system reacts is also a point of irony. If an innocent person is convicted of a crime and is incarcerated and later the true offender confesses, the innocent person is not let go immediately. It takes a year and a day to straiten this out. We have to investigate; a new trial date must be set, etc., etc. It didn't take them long to put you in when they thought you were guilty. I guess you may have the right to a speedy trial but not the right to a speedy correction.

They have even made movies exposing some of the bazaar cases. 'The Verdict' showed how a doctor with all the "big money" attorneys at his disposal tries to railroad the system for his benefit. At one point it showed that a nurse could have a copy of something she signed but because an original was produced first the copy is disregarded even though the "original" was not truly an original. It had been altered. 'And Justice for All' showed how a lawyer can know his client is guilty but can't "legally" tell the system without putting himself in trouble, especially if the guilty person is a person of prominence.

There were also many, many stories of the extreme inequities of divorce case settlements. The system began to get a little fairer primarily due to the influence of the women's lib movement. It's ironic that an initiative with its major emphasis on helping women get equality would eventually aide males.

Many movies have depicted the plight of the divorced husband and the inequities of child custody and disbursement of property. "Divorce American Style" and "Kramer vs. Kramer" are two that quickly come to mind.

The system says the woman is entitled to live "in a manner that she was accustomed to". It does not consider what the man was "accustomed" to, how about a housekeeper, a cook and a lady of the evening (once a week, whether he needs it or not) all paid for by the woman. I don't think so. Nor do they consider what the man can reasonably afford. It splits the assets in half but the man gets all the liabilities and associated bills. In child custody the system favors the woman getting custody. In general most people are in favor of the woman getting custody, but if the man is going to pay child support he should get more consideration than he actually gets. It sounds like "Taxation without representation".

In the '90s the O. J. Simpson case had America glued to the television for months. Including the actual case itself, here were so many shows that reviewed, analyzed and criticized and got anyone's and everyone's opinion on the case. All the talk shows and variety shows began to engage in the legal issues. They began to have as guests lawyers, prosecutors, ex-prosecutors, judges, ex-judges, ex-criminal lawyers, anyone that ever had anything to do with the law.

With all this publicity and the multitudes of lay people listening to all these legal experts for so long came the sense that we were all now fit for legal consulting. The whole country has since been enthralled with legalities; with cases such as Whitewater, Lewinsky, Clinton, Impeachment, in the news. This new found legal focus brought about more and more television shows that deal with legal issues. Geraldo Rivera, who frequently has "the" Marcia Clark host his show, Cochran and Company, and many of the "People's Court" type Shows. Such as Judge Joe Brown, Judge Judy, Judge Koch, Judge Mills Lane, etc.

These court room type shows allow the public to view the system, listen to other people's controversies and see the resolutions. That in and of itself is not a bad idea; however in watching many of these shows I've seen positive, negative and also some questionable behavior. Here are some elements:

1. Within the walls of the court the judge is more powerful than God.
2. Judges do not like being questioned or challenged.

3. His or her social attitude and values are the way everyone is to think and act.
4. They can make erroneous, unsubstantiated claims at any time.
5. Retorts are frowned upon.
6. You may get chastised if you try to defend yourself against the judges' statement.
7. Judges do know the law.
8. Once a judge has made up his or her mind it's all over.

What follows are a couple of examples of some negative observations.

One judge was going to take away custody of the baby of a young homeless woman. They were living in her car. By the way, it's kind of strange that the system is quick to pay a stranger more than it will give you to take care of your children. Anyway, the judge started to question the young lady as to why she could not avail herself of other options. In a rather pompous manner he said he could not see her mother could not help. Why couldn't she stay with mother? After all that is what parents are supposed to do. Well the young mother gathered herself and very sheepishly but effectively told the judge she understood his point. However, your Honor, my mother lives in the back seat! The judge was flabbergasted. To his credit his demeanor changed and he began to act more sympathetic and helpful to the young lady.

In another instance Judge Judy just by looking at one of the litigants determines and states that he is drunk. The man denies the allegation. Judge Judy asks the man's lady friend how many drinks he had that day. The lady replied one glass. The man asks what does this have to do with the case. He was correct, this was irrelevant, but again Judge Judy is in control. She asked him to leave the courtroom. She then asks the lady where he got the liquor. At the liquor store was the reply. With that arrogant, "who are you kidding" attitude Judge Judy says "you can't get a glass of liquor at the liquor store, they sell bottles." The lady points out that the man had purchased a nip. That's a single shot of liquor in a little bottle. Similar to what you might get on an airplane flight. Well Judge Judy is wrong! But she's the judge; she doesn't need to apologize, she just proceeds to her next issue or comment with that same pompous attitude.

What some people do not realize is that any financial settlements in these court cases are paid for by the television show budget. So nobody is financially burdened by whatever actions the judge decides to take. It's just entertainment. This does not take into consideration the feelings of the individuals.

The real deal is that people do not count; and poor people count even less.

The shame in it all is that there are no easily accessible checks and balances to correct the inequities and protect the people that pay the cost to have this system protect them or to keep the people we pay to administer and monitor the system honest.

Jet magazine had an article entitled "Prosecutors Violate Their Oaths by Hiding Evidence, Chicago Tribune Investigation Reveals."

A couple of writers for the Tribune did some investigation. They found hundreds of cases where prosecutors hid evidence or twisted the truth and therefore sent innocent people to prison.

"They (prosecutors) have prosecuted Black men, hiding evidence the real killers were White," Tribune writers Ken Armstrong and Maurice Possley wrote.

"They have prosecuted a wife; hiding evidence her husband committed suicide. They have prosecuted parents, hiding evidence their daughter was killed by wild dogs."
In the first study of its kind, thousands of court records, appellate rulings and lawyer disciplinary records throughout the nation were examined.

Since a 1963 U. S. Supreme Court ruling to stop misconduct by prosecutors, there have been 381 documented cases of defendants across the country who have had homicide convictions thrown out citing prosecutors concealed evidence suggesting innocence or presented evidence they knew to be false.

Although the U. S. Supreme Court has declared such acts by prosecutors as so reprehensible that it warrants criminal charges and disbarment . . . . Not one of those prosecutors was convicted of a crime. Nor were any barred from practicing law.

Instead, the prosecutors saw their careers flourish with some becoming judges or district attorneys, the Tribune said.

Also the article reported that of the 381 defendants, 67 had been sentenced to death. And nearly 30 of those 67 inmates whose cases were resolved were later freed. But almost all of them first spent at least five years in prison.

The Tribune cited various examples of how prosecutors have twisted the truth or lied. "Prosecutors have concealed evidence that discredited their star witness, pointed to other suspects or supported a defendant's claim of self defense. They have suppressed evidence that a murder occurred when the defendant had alibis . . . . In one case depicted red paint as blood. In another they portrayed hog blood as that of a human."

The Tribune reported that while it uncovered 381 wrongful homicide convictions, there are likely many other similar cases where prosecutors committed deception. "No one knows how often prosecutors engage in such duplicity but aren't caught."

"And even when prosecutors are caught, findings of misconduct aren't filed in an easily accessible directory. The legal system keeps track of convictions won, not convictions lost on appeal because prosecutors went too far." That should have read when prosecutors "break the law", "went too far" is too "soft"!

In what proves to be a justification against capital punishment a Northwestern University law professor has his students investigate capital punishment cases. They recreate the case, interview the convicted prisoners and when necessary review the testimonies with the trial informants. Some of their findings were very similar to those of the Chicago Tribune investigation. In some cases the testimonies were altered or distorted. Alibis were ignored or not presented to the jury. Eye witness testimonies twisted or "manufactured" or even paid for by the prosecution.

In all there were six cases in which the students were able to get re-trials and prove that the death row prisoners were in fact innocent. The innocent men were eventually set free but this does not excuse the ridiculous, unjust, down right unlawful process used by prosecutors. After all we are supposed to be innocent until ***proven*** guilty. The key word in these cases is proven.

This is more fuel for believers of the inequities of the Justice system. And it definitely gives credence to those who question the fairness and exactness of capital punishment within the existing system.

I would like to believe that in general and for the most part the system is fair and just but issues like these make me wonder. And as far as being Black is concerned, I think it was Richard Pryor said it best; "if you go to court looking for JUSTICE, that's what you will find, JUST US".

By the way what ever happened to "your vote counts"? What a fiasco in Florida during the Bush versus Gore presidential election. We can't even get an accurate count of votes for arguably the most important position in the world. There were dimpled chads, pregnant chads, hanging chads. Give me a break.

The Electoral College is another entity now under scrutiny. If one of the candidates gets 1 more vote than the other why should they be allotted all the electoral votes for the state? Wait, if the Electoral College delegates disagree they might not even vote for the "winner".

It makes more sense to me to divide the electoral votes up by the percentage of popular votes within the state. But again it's not about being fair, it's the Golden Rule again, he who has the gold makes the rule.

Sports

There are multitudes of "unfairness'" in the world of sports. Officials have been accused of moving the strike zone, stretching the yardage markers, counting steps between dribbles differently, etc.

One area that I still don't understand is the college ranking system and how it is administered. If the number 1 ranked team plays the number 2 ranked team you would expect the number 1 team to win. You would also expect it to be a relatively close contest. But if the number 1 team beats the number 2 team even by the slimmest of margins, guess what? The number 2 team drops way down the list to number 6 or 7 if they're lucky. You would think they could still beat the number 3 or 4 teams.

In the sixty's there was the famous Michigan State versus Notre Dame. Notre Dame was ranked number 1 and Michigan State ranked number 2. This was the last game of the season; the national championship was on the line. The game lived up to its big expectation. It was a tied score late in the game; Notre Dame had possession of the ball. They could have attempted a long field goal to try to win the game. But they opted to let the clock run out and settle for the tie. Well do you think the national ranking would be a tie? Would you think it would be awarded to the "chicken" team? Of course Notre Dame was awarded the national tittle.

The sports world is another arena that institutionalized racism festers. This is especially true at the lower levels of sports versus the professional level. The greed for money surpasses the urge to discriminate.

Often coaches tell kids that the fancy way to do things is not desired. I don't want to see any "street" ball being played. Of course the Black kids from the ghetto only knows street ball. That's how he was brought up. It seems innocent when the coach selects this but the impact on the Black kids is not addressed.

Here is a person who has played ball to impress his peers in a fashion that supports dribbling between the legs, passing behind the back and just plain showing off. Why is he now being told to change all he has learned and restricted to doing the simple things like the nice suburban kids do?

There is a long-range problem with this issue. It seems unfair to criticize a coach for wanting the players to be best at the basics and to have sound fundamentals. However, there is a restriction of creativity that can have a damaging effect on youngsters. They may not develop to their fullest or more disastrous, the youngster may quit playing altogether.

As you go higher in the sports world, the athletes themselves become aware of what is going on. I know of and have heard stories of Black ex-athletes telling potential athletes not to go out for a particular team because the coach is just going to "use" you. I've seen athletes quit teams rather than playing a lower position. They also quit because they feel restricted and/or are not allowed to play at the same time as one of their "boys".

Probably my first personal incident with what could have been racism was in high school. I was a sprinter on the track team. I ran the 50 yard dash in a holiday track meet, I came in second. Others and I thought I had won the race. A white runner was chosen the winner. Time past and I had forgotten about the race. Then one day after a track meet my track coach came over to talk to me. Joe Carey, a white man, was one of the most sincere people I have ever known. He had a photograph in his hand. Before he showed it to me, he said something very important. "There are things that are beyond your control that are going to happen during your life just because you are Black" he said. So what's new? Well he showed me the picture. It was the finish of the race I mentioned above. The picture was as decisive as you could get. There I was with the tape stretched across my chest and not broken yet and the "winner" a step behind. I was upset, but I also knew I could do nothing to change the happening. It was another experience to grow from. (And if you don't believe me I still have the picture!)

Unfortunately this was not the last time something like this happened to me. In college I ran in a championship meet at MIT. Again I thought I had won the race. This time I was picked for third place. Boy was I miffed. Well, the newspaper the next day had a picture of the finish of the dash. The caption read that I had won. It certainly looked that way in the picture. No Change, I was still third in the books.

I know I am not the only person that this has happened to. It's also factual that this has happened to white athletes too. But if we were to tally up the numbers, the scale would be unbalanced against the Black athlete.

The Olympics is an example of the inequities of the "system". In 1968 two Black athletes, Tommie Smith and John Carlos, decided to make a "political" statement on the winners platform. They wanted the world to know that even though it the United States of America is the best country in the world, there were "unequal" and racial injustices occurring. After their demonstration they were told to leave the Olympic compound. "This was not the forum to air our dirty laundry" was the cry. How dare you use this athletic event for a political statement?

As the 1980 Olympics drew near, the issue of using this athletic event for a political statement turned completely around. The Games were to be conducted in Russia. Now remember the Olympics are not supported financially by the US government at all. Only individual and corporate money is used. But the US government, against the wishes of the athletes and many sports supporters, decided that the US would not compete in Russia. So athletes, some of whom would never again get this opportunity, were denied the right to compete. This is a double standard if I've ever seen one.

Baseball's 'vicinity' play at second base is really contradictory. If a fielder misses a tag or a base by 1 inch any other time the runner is safe. But at second base at the front end of a double play, the fielder just needs to be 'in the vicinity' of the bag. The runner is out. Vicinity as I have seen it means; 2-3 feet at best.

Also in baseball you frequently hear the announcer explain how if the pitcher were getting his OTHER pitches over the plate maybe they would call those pitches strikes. I thought the strike zone defined what a strike was not how the pitcher is doing on the other pitches.

Hockey! Fighting is not part of the game. You must be kidding! It's the only sport in which you can fight and stay in or return to the game. A friend said, "what a great game. You can get in a fight, sit down for 5 minutes, get up and start all over". Fighting *is* part of the game. For some people it is the whole game.

Another issue in hockey is the dropping of the puck during a face-off. A player from each team is poised with their hockey sticks read to direct the puck to one of his teammates. It's a very tense moment. After all you want to get the puck for your team. The puck is then dropped and the battle for control begins. But wait! The official fakes the drop and then signals either or both of the players out of the circle. There is no recourse nor is there any explanation required. The official just does it at his whim when he wants to, like it or not. Another show of how authority goes to peoples head. Can't say it's not fair, the official has the "right" to do it. But I think it's ridiculous.

In football it is considered a penalty for a quarterback to throw the ball away to avoid a sack—intentional grounding penalty. But if time is running out the same guy takes the ball from the center and immediately spikes the ball to stop the clock. That's considered a good play. You should be able to throw the ball away or not.

The professional basketball, baseball and football leagues certainly have their share of controversy with racism. The infiltration of black coaches, managers, officials and front office people has not nearly kept pace with the involvement of the black athlete in the sports. Even the ability of black athletes to play the "smart, leadership" positions took longer to occur in the pros than it did at the college level. You mean Black athletes can lead their high school and college teams to championships but can't do it in the pros? They can be great players but cannot coach or manage?

Take a look at the sports programs all over the networks, even though Black athletes have been dominant in sports they don't seem to be able to speak for or analyze their sport at the same percentage of involvement as their white counterparts. This imbalance also has the effect of allowing some unintentional biased opinions and perspectives.

The 1998 NBA **LOCKOUT** is an example in point. The media played into the ordeal as though the players were striking for more money. Of course most of the players are Black and most of the owners are White. Also the fact that the owners pay the media and control the money has a naturally biasing effect on the outlook.

The fans were asked what they thought. Many said they did not care if the NBA ever played again. Many commented on how greedy the players were. Some did mention that the owners were greedy too, but most of the emphasis was on the players.

I emphasized LOCKOUT because it was just that, a lockout. What really happened was that the owners had been pricing themselves out of the market. In their greed to have the best players and the best teams they had been increasing the players contracts over and over again. The time had come when they could not only not afford to continue, but wanted to go back and renegotiate a low overall pay structure for the entire league. When the players refused the pay cut, the owners LOCKED THEM OUT. It was not a strike. But if you ask most fans or the general public they would probably say it was a player strike. The predominantly Black athletes are portrayed as the bad boys again.

And then there's Tiger. Golf has been a large part of the sports scene in the US and the world for quite some time. Arnold Palmer's success and style were mainly responsible for its rejuvenation especially here in America. Then came the "Golden Bear" Jack Nicklaus with a dominance and determination never seen before.

This brought out questions like: Who was the best ever? Is Nicklaus better than Palmer, Byron Nelson, and Ben Hogan? Who was the best amateur ever?

There were few arguments as to whether or not golf was a sport.

Along comes Eldrick "Tiger" Woods and the questions and comments begin to show the true "*colors*" of the American golfing and non-golfing people.

Let it be know that Earl and Kultida Woods were great parents. They did all the right things to prepare their son for life in the US of A. He was spiritually, mentally and physically "loved". He had excellent schooling and coaching. And he was given the alternatives, pros and cons. As he grew old enough he was allowed to make his own decisions as to his future in golf.

As an amateur, Tiger won three consecutive Junior United States Golf Association tittles. He then went on to win three consecutive Amateur United States Golf Association tittles before turning professional. One of his trademarks happened to be a fist pumping gesture as he made long putts or won a hole or tournament. This was not unusual for youngsters, after all he was still a teenager, but the older, more traditional golfers took offence to this "football", "basketball" type of celebration on the sophisticated golf course. The irony of it all is that Tiger was as mature, mannered, sophisticated and "polished" a teenager as you would want to see.

Then the other questions came. Is he Black or what? Tiger's ancestry is multi-racial and it does include Black. Tiger prefers not to exclude any of his heritage and therefore does not claim to be just one of "anything". Well people began to attack this aspect early in his career. Because of the proper preparing by his parents, Tiger was able to get past this petty stuff with no distraction from his focus, to be the best golfer ever.

As Tiger's professional career began to take off there were other attempts to "sabotage" his success. He won the Masters. They began to talk about changing the course to make it more difficult. Or was that to make it Tiger proof. Tiger won 6 consecutive tournaments, a feat not done in years. An article in a local paper starts a discussion. Is golf a sport or is it just a game. Let's compare Tiger to Michael Jordan as an athlete. See he's not that good. Give me a break!! I didn't here these ridiculous comparisons for Palmer or Nicklaus. There was no challenge as to whether Jack could beat Ted Williams at tennis.

This shows the underlying racism that still exists in the United States today.

School

School experiences also fit the unfair is OK but this is ridiculous situation. Take for instance the issue of separation of church and state.

There's all the violence going on in the street. The abuse of children has been growing more and more rampart. Sportsmanship is declining at a very raid pace sexual promiscuity causing more unwed mothers and single parent homes. The moral fiber of the country is at an all time low.

It is obvious that the school environment has a big influence on the value system and the judgements of our youth. Children actually spend more time in the early, formative years in the classroom than they spend at home with their families. They learn about peer pressure, this is their first dealing with non-parental authority figures and issues. Remember kindergarten? This is probably the first time in our lives we are asked to sit still for longer than 10 minutes. What do you mean I have to raise my hand to go to the bathroom? Why don't we get more time to eat? I want more recess. Yes this is a most influential time in our lives.

Why then in this "one Nation, UNDER GOD" is there such a furor over prayer in the classroom. By the way don't we *have* to say the Pledge Allegiance to the Flag before class every day? It seems it's OK to teach sex education, punishment, politics, etc. but prayer is a no no. Something is wrong with this picture. I don't say that we must dictate how much or which religion; or that children be forced against their or their parents whishes to pray. But it seems to me that any time we can allow or show others the proper, correct, right, righteous, sensitive way of being and doing, it can't be wrong.

If we look back carefully at our school experiences we will probably find the first instances of life's inequities. Teacher's pets give us our first exposure to favoritism. We can't seem to understand why we try so hard, do all our work and watch "the pet" get a better grade, extra cookies, and special assignments instead of us.

We also learn how the whole group can get punished for the bad acts of just a few. This comes fast on the heals of the learnings around not "snitching". If nobody squeals on the bad guy or gal all are punished. If you squeal on the bad guy or gal, the teacher punishes them. But, you may receive a much harder "punishment" from the culprits. It's not fair. But it turns out to be more like what life's about than we care to imagine.

When you do all your work you will get your just reward right. Wrong! You do all the homework, have 100% attendance, participate in class discussions, get 90-100 on all tests and quizzes. You get an A for the course, correct. No!! Professor X does not give out A's to anyone. Who the H___ is he or she? Well the dean says "it's the professor's class. I can't change the grade." That's not the general practice but their certainly are enough of these "ridiculous" professors around to make life difficult for too many of us.

Another similar issue is when Professor Y flunks half the class; just because. There is no reasonable reason given. You talk to the dean of the department. You know the one with all the power in the world. The dean says—"I understand the wrongdoing and it doesn't make sense to me, but I can't change the grade".

The Negro

In Black society today there are many major struggles going on. Some of the topics are leadership, economics, affirmative action, identity and survival.

The issue of leadership has been in limbo since the assassination of Dr. Reverend Martin Luther King. Malcolm X was leading the Black Muslim effort at around the same time. He was expanding his Muslim following and wrestling leadership from Elija Mohamed. Malcolm was an ex-convict and of the militant nature. This provided Blacks with rebellious and violent feelings an alternative to the non-violent philosophy Martin preached and lived. Between the two they covered most of the needs for Black leadership. The improvements of that generation seemed to be very apparent. Integration became more widespread, Black awareness improved; Blacks began to "grow" in both the corporate world and society in general.

It has long been a contention of many Blacks that in order to achieve our maximum effect and realize our economic success, we had to relate with Africa, the Mother land. The irony of this "relationship" is, Africans who come to America from Africa, don't seem to want to be identified as "one of us". They are not "Negroes". That is, they are not Black Americans.

I personally have come to dislike the term African-American. I think it eludes the truth. Those of us born in America, especially if we are second or third generation Americans, have been as much a part of the making of this country as anyone. We are Americans. Yes we are of African decent, but never the less Americans.

Truly if they have become American citizens Hakeem Olajuwon and Dikembe Mutombo are African Americans. In my mind to distinguish their ethnic backgrounds from our ethnic backgrounds there would have to be some other term or phrase to describe us.

Besides if Ernie Els or Gary Player, two White South Africans, were to become United States citizens and have offspring, what would we call them? They'd be African-Americans? But they are White. And what do we call Yannick Noah the Black French tennis player? He's not an American but we would try to label him incorrectly as an African American. And what about the Armatraj brothers who are tennis players from India? They have extremely dark skin color. Would they be called African-Americans if they were to become United States citizens?

If we want to give in to society's need to identify everyone's ethnic background of distinction then call us Negroes. My definition of Negro is "Black Americans of African decent that have been stripped of their heritage and culture and has developed a heritage and culture within this country".

If we take this philosophy and unite as Negroes we can establish a leadership and identity in America. This identity allows for political growth, social unity and the establishment of an economic base that we can control.

One of the benefits is the ability to provide a unified culture and leadership for other people of color to relate to when they come to America. This is similar to the culture and unity we see when visiting Bermuda, the Bahamas, Barbados, Cape Verde, etc. All are places primarily inhabited by people of color. These places all have different cultures but when you visit it is apparent who the people are. They are all proud of the culture that they are living in. That is not to say they disown their African ancestry and do not maintain "distant" relationship with Africa, they do. But the key here is to first recognize and be proud of the culture you live in now.

I believe this lack of Black American distinction has detracted from the effectiveness of affirmative action for Blacks in this country. We have allowed the effort to be "watered down" by including Hispanics, Asians, etc. Don't get me wrong, everyone is entitled to equal opportunity, but affirmative action is different.

Affirmative action should be limited to the people who were brought to this country against their will, stripped of their culture, separated from their families and made to do all the manual labor that made this country what it is today.

The other minorities came to this country of their own volition looking for opportunity. Nothing is wrong with that but they have not, in my mind, earned the special need of affirmative action.

Statistics have always been used to identify and "justify" some of the stigmatism's associated with the Black man. Percent of the population, how many in the workforce, numbers committing crimes, etc. The numbers associated with crimes is a perfect example of the old adage "figures never lie, but liars do figure". Numbers are only as good as the method and soundness of the process.

The example that comes to mind is that of shoplifting.

For years we have been told "the majority of shoplifting is done by Black people". The statistics are brought out to "prove" the statement. 60-70% of those caught shoplifting are Black.

Here's the deal. 12,000 people shop at the mall. There are 10,000 whites and 2,000 Black consumers. There are 200 Black people caught stealing and 100 whites. This means twice as many Blacks are stealing versus whites. Or put another way, 10 times as many Blacks are stealing; 10% versus 1% right. The numbers do not lie.

Oh no!! Here's what **really** happens!

Of the 10,000 white shoppers only about 200 or 2% are watched or followed by security. Thus 50% of those observed are caught stealing.

Of the 2,000 Black shoppers at least 1,500 (75%) are watched and followed by security. In fact the security team is told specifically to do this. This means that about 13% of those observed are caught stealing.

This makes the statistics look quite different. Now if you look at the OBSERVED numbers, only 13% of Blacks are stealing as opposed to 50% of whites.

I realize that all store do not follow the same procedures. But, a sufficient number of stores in the area that I live do follow this inequity.

The proof is in the pudding.

Here is a real life story that shows not only how ridiculous this is, but also how obviously flawed the "system" can be and how aware of the inequities some of the opportunists are.

Five white teen-age friends were going to the sporting goods store in the mall. They asked a young Black friend to go with them. He agreed and went with them. When they got to the store the Black youngster went into the store first. He had a specific article in mind that he wanted to purchase. The white friends went on about their business in a different direction.

As usual, one of the store plain cloths detectives began to follow the Black male around. The young Black male began to notice. He became so upset that he left the store without making his purchase. Meanwhile the white males were about their business.

They all returned to the car. The Black youth noticed the white friends were taking things from their pockets and from under their shirts. He asks, "What's going on?" The white youth told him the deal.

"We invited you because we know the security people will follow you. When they do that lets us take what we want. They're watching you not us."
Remember, this is a true story!

Not only do the statistics lie and the Black men get a bad rap. But, the stores loose business. The Black man left disgusted without purchasing what he came for. And the white males took what they came for without paying for the items.

Another real life story: This shows the same kind of issue of how white people play the stereotypes to their advantage, and the system "obliges".

Years ago in Boston a man called the police and claimed a Black male pulled a gun on he and his wife. The story goes on that the Black man shot and killed the woman and wounded him. A search was started for a Black male with the typical features dressed in the typical garb. A Black suspect was apprehended. Naturally he had a previous record. The capture was now viable, the crime solved. Wrong!!

As it turns out, the man who called police had conspired with his brother and killed his own wife. The alibi was concocted for a cover-up. It almost worked.

One side note: Even though the Black male was innocent of these charges because he had a previous record he was not released immediately and there were no ramifications to the police for a false arrest. That's really ridiculous.

An interesting view on this subject was posed shortly after the Columbine High School misfortune.

Let me tell you about my parallel universe.

It may exist in the same physical space as, say, my racially desegregated world of work. But it is a separate emotional place shared almost exclusively by other blacks.

We may see the same things as whites, but we often experience them quite differently. Take the shootings at Columbine High in Littleton, Colo. In my parallel world, you hear comments like, "I'm so glad those killers weren't black. You know we'd all be in trouble if they were."

This is not just to say that a certain shame is associated with black misbehavior. In the parallel universe, there is acute awareness that white America responds differently when killers are black and that its police apparatus can easily become a Gestapo-like operation—as occurred in the aftermath of Susan Smith's claim that a black man had kidnapped her two white toddlers in South Carolina.

In that infamous 1994 case, black men were being detained in six states while Smith's boys sat strapped in a car at the bottom of a pond where she'd left them.

In Columbine, the parents of the killers were not questioned by police for several hours after the crimes, even though police knew that bombs had been made in their homes. Had the killers been black, the parents would no doubt have been hauled off in handcuffs in front of television cameras, and everybody who knew them would be under suspicion.

In my world, you also hear, "The chickens have come home to roost."

There is a feeling that if more attention had been paid to America's "culture of violence" when it appeared to be confined to the inner city, these rural and suburban school shootings might have been prevented.

"Why are all the mass murderers middle-class white men and boys?" Apart from the notion that black and white boys have different styles of aggression due to different ways of being socialized, there is a belief in the parallel universe that as America loses its "status" as a white nation in the next century, more and more white people will be going insane.

In Columbine, a TV reporter actually referred to one of the killers as "a gentleman who drove a BMW." The shooters also were referred to as members of a "clique," not a gang, and they were—we were reminded again and again—so full of academic promise.

This obvious identification with the killers, and the reluctance to demonize them as blacks would have been, did not go over well in the parallel universe.

"As the media tries to soften the racist element in this tragedy," came an e-mail from Asiba Tupahache, in New York, "one student in the library said she heard them laugh after shooting the black young athlete and said, 'Oh, look! You can see his brains.' With that kind of attitude, these guys could have had lucrative careers in the NYPD."

Writing for the Baltimore Afro American newspaper, columnist Wiley A. Hall 3rd recalled America's knee-jerk response to gun violence when it was being portrayed as unique to urban areas. "Politicians talked about the need to crack down on what they described as tough young urban hoodlums who are terrorizing the city," he wrote. "Sociologists blamed negligent urban parents who fail to instill civilized values in their children. Police promised to make more arrests. Prosecutors promised more convictions. And judges promised to send more teenaged offenders to do hard time in adult institutions."

Now, in the aftermath of Columbine, the finger is being pointed at "a culture of alienation," and there is talk of improving school curriculums, controlling guns, regulating the Internet and installing V-chips in our TVs.

It's not just that it looks like excuses are being made for the killers at Columbine; it's that some of them are the same ones that were so roundly rejected when used to explain violence among blacks. The one about how the killers' status as outcasts was to blame really struck a nerve.

"Those of us whose high school experiences also included being racialized have a more compounded view of this kind of labeling, discrimination and outcasting," Tupahache wrote. "Only our visible resistance made them drug us, call us troubled, got us abruptly reprimanded, kicked out with no questions asked. Others can wear swastikas, make disturbed videos and show it in class and all is quiet."

Such feelings and concerns from the parallel universe occasionally break out into the other world.

In the New York Times on Friday, Harvard sociologist Orlando Patterson lamented that "there is a disturbing double standard in the way we discuss the problems of different groups of people and in the way we label deviant behavior. If the terrorist act of white, middle-class teenagers creates an orgy of national soul-searching, then surely the next time a heinous crime is committed by underclass African-American or Latino kids, we should engage in the same kind of national self-examination."

His was an eloquent appeal for love and understanding in a world where justice is truly colorblind. In my parallel universe, however, we aren't holding our breath.

Copyright 1999 the Washington Post Company

One additional "figures don't lie, but liars figure" statistical malpractice occurs in the movie business. Often Black folks wonder why it is that the Black movies do not play at the local theaters very long. After all most of us want and do frequent the theater to see *our* latest masterpiece. Well this is how we are duped into thinking that the Black films have low box office success.

When we go to the movie theater we don't see the film we wish to see advertised on the marquee. Some of us just assume it is gone or was listed in the paper as a mistake and leave. No credit for viewers. If we are persistent we go home and call the theater or the newspaper. Or we ask the management before we leave the movie. They tell us the movie is playing in the back show room but we haven't had time to post it on the marquee or to print the tickets. They give you a ticket with the name of some other film. They tell you to present this to the ticket taker and all is going to be OK. You do get to see the movie, however the credit for box office attraction is now given to the other film.

Wonder why Black films and actors and actresses are not as successful as you would think they should be? Or that there aren't as many Black films list on marquees as we think there should be?

Another trick of the system

Love

Love is probably the most individualistic and intriguing issue in life. The fact that it is virtually indefinable gives us no yardstick to measure each definition. We tend to think that others should feel the same way we do. The sexual harassment dilemma of recent years really brings the issue of interpretation to the forefront. Women began to register complaints against the boss, co-workers, peers, co-students, teachers, doctors, dentists, etc, etc, etc. Accusations were not just leveled by women, men also cried "fowl" on occasion.

Nobody was exempt from the list of harassers. The two most controversial "harassers" have been parents and men of the cloth. Ministers and priests have been accused and even convicted of sexually molesting young boys. Some of the offenses were enacted in the church. These are not issues for debate. There is no doubt these are criminal acts.

On the other hand, there are cases of harassment that are questionable. Many women complained about actions that had been going on for some time. There were many cases in which the women even participated in some of the action. As their peers began to make the world aware of the injustices, some began to change their tune. What had been a joke or innocent tease or flirting were now grounds for legal action. What was OK yesterday is trouble today.

Men began to fear just giving sincere compliments. Just a "Gee you look nice today" could get you in trouble. I remember a manager at a diversity meeting explaining a similar dilemma. One of the women had on a very pretty outfit. He told us that he wanted to compliment her on the outfit. But especially because he was a manager he resisted taking the risk.

Isn't it ridiculous when a person feels guilty or feels it's risky to say something good to someone? After all, don't we dress up and, especially women fix ourselves to look good?

Now don't misunderstand, I realize there are lots of substantiated claims and harassment cases that have caused lasting psychological effects on people. There have been very public cases that have raised eyebrows and caused many debates. The Clarence Thomas Anita Hill case is probably the most famous.

There have also been criminal investigations of some very famous people with the underlying issue of harassment.

This has put a strain on the man woman relationship. It has become more of a challenge to "meet" someone. You have to approach the opposite sex with caution.

There is also the old issue that women have always said that men think with their penis. In many cases the accusation has merit. But to stereotype all men is definitely wrong. To take it to the next step, what about the women? Who does more ogling and screaming and "drooling" over the heartthrob of the time? Just mention the name of the movie star, TV star, athlete, singer or any form of entertainer in the presence of women and listen to the noise. Just what are they thinking with?

The Black race has had an even tougher challenge in the "sexual revolution". The Black female is "fighting" both the female revolution as well as establishing an identity of her own. The Black males plight against the racism has not been successful enough for us to "be in control" of our destiny. This has driven the Black female to attempt to establish her own control. The side effect has been a challenging relationship between Black men and women. The system adds to this challenge by selectively giving Black women preference over Black men. This gives corporate America 2 hits for the price of 1 in the diversity tally. A tick is given both for being a woman and another for being a Black.

Over the years the there have been some controversial plays, books and movies about Black women that have been jilted by their men. My belief is that this controversy is supported and condoned by the system. There are a disproportionate number of these types of plays and movies compared to similar plots about white males and white women. As a matter of fact I cannot remember too many such movies. The ones that I do recall are comedies and not serious movies. This comedy flavor gives it a different impact.

The challenge has brought about what I call the "SISTER" attitude. Black women have taken on the "aura" of the Black movement of the 60's and 70's when we were "Brothers". The difference is that the sisters have somewhat alienated themselves from the brothers. Young Black females are told by their mothers not to let the brother get in the way of your success. You can do it by yourself. You don't need him. He's only interested in one thing.

I have watched a few of the daytime talk shows that have addressed this issue. The topic of one was "Why can't Black women find a good Black man?" One of the main reasons given was that good Black men go after white women. It was interesting to listen to the audience's opinions and to watch the body language as the tough questions were posed.

One young Black man stated his contention. "Every time I meet a Black woman I may be interested in she has an attitude. She makes me feel that it is not a relationship we're looking at but a battle. She wants me to know that she doesn't need me. I have my own thing going on. This attitude turns him off".

A young Black female in the audience stood up and emphatically told all "If you can't deal with the fact that I know I'm good and I have it going on, that's your problem!" Unfortunately the host of the show did not point out that this is just the "attitude" the young man was talking about. You don't have to challenge someone as soon as you meet him or her. It's the "walking around with a chip on your shoulder" syndrome.

It's nice to see camaraderie. It is also important to believe in yourself and have a sense of direction. But we must remember that "No man is an island unto himself" or "herself". Life's too short for us to expend so much energy arguing with each other, trying to protect ourselves from the "enemy" and just plain acting like children. Why must the most enjoyable be so challenging? Why can't we just get along?

It's ironic that the pets in our lives give us more than we give each other. They meet you at the door when you come home. No mater how you feel or how you treat them, the pouch will still wants to greet you as if it were the last time. And we are supposed to be the most intelligent animal? The real animals know what unconditional love is. If only we could learn from them.

There have been some rather serious charges recently brought against little school children. I am referring to the sexual harassment charges against kids under 10 years old. It's strange that in a world that is trying to get away from violence, we penalize little kids for giving kisses to their peers of the opposite sex. Remember we're talking an age that they probably can't even spell harassment let alone know what it is.

Politics

During the 2008-2009 presidential campaign like most Black Americans I paid more attention to politics than I had ever done in my life. The once before unmentionable thought that a Black man could become president of the United States of America had more than just credibility. There was a trace of reality. In the end it was the culmination of the years of sacrifice, bitterness and mistreatment that goes along with striving for equality as the minority. I and many others that I talked with never thought we would see the likes of this in our lifetime. Barack Obama was nominated by a major party and subsequently became the first Black President of the United States of America. Pinch me. I'm not sure I believe it.

That space of time was filled with many highs and lows. And for me some real eye opening events and issues. To watch as the Black candidate had to fend off the typical attacks on his character, ethics, dedication, knowledge, awareness, strength, religion, loyalty, his past acquaintances and worst of all his Americanism. "Where's his birth certificate? "—give me a break.

But the "underdog" had done what we as Blacks have had to do all our lives. Dot all the Is, cross all the Ts anticipate the attacks and put together a team to pull off what is not expected of us. He was very convincing to say the least. And as Blacks were always taught when we were growing up to do everything we do in a respectful manner. Despite Barack's respectfulness his opposition got down right nasty at times.

This nastiness continued into his presidency. Insinuations, misrepresentations, name calling etc. continued. Things like, "Obama Care", "death panels", socialist, Muslim were commonly used as negative issues of the president.

We know people of one political party might vote for the opposition. Although there is no way to confirm that publicly endorsing the "opposition" is an extremely rare but publicly open event. I don't remember ever seeing a "prominent" person of one political party endorse a presidential candidate of the opposing party. Colin Powell and Michael Smerconish and others openly endorsed Barack. The reasoning had to do with the character of the man and respectful campaign he ran along with his "political" agenda.

Irony of the administrations and continue attacks:

During the eight year G. W. Bush administration the US government spending was out of control, they did not budget for nor account for the spending associated with the Iraq war, they reduced taxes for the upper income "rich" wage earners and basically let Wall Street run out of control. After years of diminishing returns in an effort to stave off a recession they implemented a stimulus program.

The Obama administration in its first year tried to implement programs, regulations, etc. to "stop the bleeding". The republicans did nothing but criticize and refuse to cooperate: even if it was the same process the Bush administration implemented or suggested. Stimulus program, trial of terrorist in criminal vs. military court, etc., etc., etc.

Obama met the fallen soldiers in the middle of the night and was accused of "making it a photo op".

Instead of making a hasty decision on sending more troops to Afghanistan Obama studied the situation, got inputs from all concerned and pondered the thoughts of more fallen soldiers from his first hand meeting at the air field.

The economists agree that the bail-outs of the major banks and auto corporations were necessary to keep the country afloat. The republicans heavily criticized this as "us bankrupting our grand children". No mention that these were loans to be paid back. No owning up to the fact that their spending would have the same effect.

During his 8 years as president George W. Bush spent more time on vacation than any previous president. He also had an unwritten rule that he was to get at least 8 hours of sleep. I guess this is understandable for his age, but not for the position. After all he chose to run, he had some idea of the demands—his father was president, wasn't he watching?

The irony of this is that Barack Obama was criticized (by the same republicans that surrounded Bush) for taking vacation at such a critical time.

In the same vein Obama has been accused of trying to do too much at one time. His efforts on health care reform are interfering with homeland security. Maybe it's because they got used to Bush and didn't think a president could walk and chew gum at the same time. Damned if you do, damned if you don't.

The republicans have also accused Obama of waiting too long to address the public in regards to an airline terrorist attack. He responded in 3 days, Bush took 6 days. Then one prominent republican stated that all the homeland terrorist attacks since 9/11 were on Obama's watch. Referring to 2 airlines related terrorist attacks, they both failed; one was the "underwear" bomber (December 2009) and the other the infamous "shoe" bomber (December 2001). It may seem to some that Obama has been in office for a long time but that's ridicules. He also failed to "remember" the anthrax and at least 3 other terrorist issues on the homeland after 9/11.

Guantanamo Bay presents another of those republican "memory lapse" issues. When the interrogations and bad photos issues went public there was a republican outcry to close the detention facility. Now that Barack has put that on his agenda the republicans say it's a bad idea and it threatens our homeland security. Make up your minds! Or do you have any?

Rush Limbaugh, a republican far right conservative, has been an opponent of the Obama administration and anything they propose. He is famous for his stance of wanting to see "Obama fail". Specifically in opposition to the need for health care reform.

Recently Rush was treated in Hawaii for a medical issue. Upon his release he concluded that "based on the treatment he received there is nothing wrong with the US medical care system". Evidently it's irrelevant that he can afford and has health care insurance, he was in Hawaii were health care insurance is mandatory and he is (I say this reluctantly) a prominent person. This ignores the facts of the number of Americans that don't have, can't afford or have preconceived conditions that exempt them from medical insurance.

During the primary campaign Sarah Palin is asked simple questions about what she reads or what she knows or doesn't know about foreign politics. These are depicted as "hard" questions. Clearly documented changes in Sarah's stances on issues have her supporters sighting it as harassing and mistreatment by the press.
And when Sarah resigns her governorship because I think she said it was getting out of hand she's not a quitter?

I think these people that say these ridiculous things and make ridiculous allegations don't seem to realize that the electronics boom has allowed us to tape, video and audio, and save information for years. All we have to do is replay the tapes and you will see the BOLD FACE LIES of these people. The scary thing is quite a few of them are in very influential positions in government.

In the past the general, though unpublished, rule of order was that you never criticized our president especially in a public forum.

Boy has that changed.

Everything that Obama does gets ridiculed like the office of the president has never see.

Can you believe a president could believe getting criticized for addressing the students of the country about the need to get an education?

How about getting berated for writing a book addressed to kids regarding the same issue.

As mentioned above he even got bad reviews for greeting the fallen soldiers as their coffins were brought back to the country from the war.

Are these real concerns or are they just a combination of partisan views and pure racism?

TEA PARTY

The tea party movement does nothing more than add more fuel to the fire. They have some legitimate issues as all people do, but the language they use, the tactics they propose and the rhetoric they use suggest more than just policy opposition.

We want our country back. From who? The Black man? Are you Native American Indians? Because if you're not why would you assume this is your country anyhow?

The proof is in the pudding. A tea party winning candidate that was in opposition to the government taking over and running everything got upset that he had to wait for his medical benefits to take effect until he was sworn in. All of a sudden he wanted the government to step in and give him his benefits immediately.

What hypocrisy!!!

The auto bail-out of General Motors proved not only successful bur profitable to the taxpayers. GM paid back the "LOAN" with interest, the stock went public, jobs in Michigan increased and Obama was again criticized for failure.

Sometimes I think we're watching a different world.

The Finally

Just when you think it's all coming together; the calm before the storm; it's a piece of cake from here on in; I'm over the hump; it's time to relax and enjoy the rest of your life; "UP POPS THE DEVIL".

I worked for Polaroid Corporation for over 30 years. I had assignments in over a dozen locations in Cambridge, Waltham and Norwood, and in at least as many departments of the company, Facilities, Plant Engineering, Optics, Robotics Assembly, Production, Service, etc., etc., etc. Participated in most of the corporate initiatives; vertical council, Intercultural work shop, work redesign, re-engineering, Total Quality Ownership facilitation, Affirmative Action Committee, Energy Conservation Committee, to name a few.

It was a great family atmosphere type of company. Good pay, growth opportunity, challenging assignments, good benefits, great people and what we all thought was an good, reliable retirement/severance plan.

Over the past 10 years or so with the challenge of digital technology to the instant photography arena Polaroid has fallen on some hard financial times. In the last 5 years specifically the company has drastically changed its corporate officers and its emphasis from technical to marketing. The stock went down dramatically and Polaroid began to "restructure", that is downsize quickly. So when my boss told me that my job function was no longer needed I was not very surprised.

After all with over 30 years of service and age 55 in quick sight and a severance plan that would give me 24 weeks pay and cross me over into retirement benefits, hey I'm OK with that.

Well here I am asking if my first severance check will be direct deposit or a separate check. Oh, if you had direct deposit that's what it'll be. HOWEVER, people have been calling in this morning complaining that they have not received their checks. This is a minor glitch right? WRONG.

Next day: POLAROID CORPORATION FILES FOR CHAPTER 11 BANKRUPTCY PROTECTION. No severance payment agreements will be honored; all retirees medical and life insurance benefits have been cancelled.

You would think the court would not put the little guy in the same pot as the big banks and bondholders but it looks like that's just what they did.

To add insult to injury less than 2 months later they're in front of the court asking for retaining bonuses for "key" executives. You know the guys that ran the company into chapter 11; Executives with no place to go anyway.

A little insight on how the "system" works for them and against you. Polaroid makes this announcement on the 6th of the month. We want to object to these payments. Well the deadline for filing an objection is the 3rd of that month; even if you want to object you can't, the process does not give you the timely information to be effective.

The other issue about major corporations filing for bankruptcy protection is they are incorporated in Delaware. The federal bankruptcy courts are in Wilmington, Delaware. The logistics for filing claims, getting information and/or petitioning objections or any other issues is in the favor of the major institutions.

I'd like to think the "system" would protect the little man, but the reality is the same old golden rule is in effect. He, who has the gold, makes the rules.

Conclusion

I hope this book has been thought provoking. Some of the incidents, thoughts, ideas and issues can be viewed in a comical fashion. But, for the most part they are serious and can have a profound impact on all of our lives.

How we talk to each other, how we treat each other, how we remember each other is not always as cut and dry or as clear as we might think.

We all see things from various perspectives and need to take time to here and understand the other's perspectives. Life is so short. We do not need to spend too much time battling over insignificant things.

For me two statements say it best:
A Gandhi quote,

"An eye for an eye makes the whole world blind"

and

The Serenity prayer,

> *"God give me the serenity to accept things I cannot change,*
> *The courage to change the things I can and*
> *The wisdom to know the difference."*